Martial Arts

Karate Blocks

by Stuart Schwartz
and Craig Conley

Consultant:
Mark Willie, Instructor
Central Minnesota Karate
Mankato State University

CAPSTONE
HIGH/LOW BOOKS
an imprint of Capstone Press
Mankato, Minnesota

Capstone High/Low Books are published by Capstone Press
818 North Willow Street • Mankato, MN 56001
http://www.capstone-press.com

Library of Congress Cataloging-in-Publication Data
Schwartz, Stuart, 1945–
Karate blocks/by Stuart Schwartz and Craig Conley.
p. cm.—(Martial arts)
Includes bibliographical references (p. 44) and index.
Summary: A general description of karate, including its origins and
development, warm-up exercises, basic and advanced blocks, and safety
aspects.
ISBN 0-7368-0008-5
1. Karate—Juvenile literature. [1. Karate.] I. Conley, Craig, 1965– . II. Title.
III. Series: Martial arts (Mankato, Minn.)
GV1114.3.S35 1999
796.815'3—dc21
                                                    98-19594
                                                       CIP
                                                       AC

Editorial Credits

Cara Van Voorst, editor; James Franklin, cover designer and illustrator;
  Sheri Gosewisch, photo researcher

Photo Credits

All photographs by Gallery 19/Gregg R. Andersen.

Table of Contents

Chapter 1

Karate for Defense

Karate means empty hand in Japanese. In karate, karate-ka use their hands and feet as weapons. A karate-ka is a student of karate. Karate-ka perform kicks, punches, strikes, and blocks.

Many people learn karate for self-defense. Self-defense is the act of protecting oneself. Some people practice karate for exercise.

People of all ages can learn karate. But students should make sure they are healthy enough for training. They should check with doctors before they take lessons.

The Origin of Karate
Karate is a martial art. A martial art is a type of self-defense or fighting. Many martial arts

Many people learn karate for self-defense.

Some karate-ka practice outside.

come from Asia. Karate was developed on
Okinawa Island near Japan in the 1600s.
Different people in Okinawa developed their
own styles of karate. Today, people can study
many karate styles. The movements described
in this book are Shotokan style.

Gichin Funakoshi developed the Shotokan style of karate. The Emperor of Japan asked Funakoshi to open a school in 1922. Funakoshi taught Shotokan karate to many Japanese people. He died in 1957. Karate schools still teach the Shotokan style of karate today. Many karate-ka call Funakoshi the Father of Modern Karate.

A sensei (SEN-say) named Oshima brought karate to North America in 1955. Sensei is the Japanese word for teacher.

Some people practice karate as a sport. Today, many people train for karate competitions. Karate-ka can test their skills against other students at competitions.

Where Karate-ka Practice

Karate-ka can practice in any open space. Some karate-ka practice outside or in large rooms at home. But most karate-ka practice at karate schools called dojos.

Each dojo has a large, open room. The walls of this room have mirrors. Karate-ka

need the open space to perform basic karate movements. Karate-ka can see if their positions are correct in the mirrors. They can move their bodies to the correct positions.

Karate Blocks
A block is a karate move for defense. Karate-ka use their arms for most blocks. They move their arms to block kicks, strikes, and punches from their opponents. An opponent is someone against whom a karate-ka is fighting. Successful blocks protect the body from injuries. Injury means harm to the body.

All blocks can keep kicks, punches, and strikes from harming the body. Some blocks absorb a blow. This means a karate-ka takes a blow with his arms. But the best blocks deflect blows. A karate-ka steps aside and pushes a blow aside to deflect it.

Karate-ka practice their movements in front of mirrors.

Chapter 2

Getting Ready to Practice

Karate-ka should warm up before each workout. A good warm-up may prevent injuries to joints or muscles.

Most karate-ka wear gi (GEE) during practice. A gi is a loose-fitting cotton uniform. Shotokan karate-ka wear white gi. The gi have belts. Karate-ka at different levels of karate skill wear belts of different colors. Beginning students wear white belts. The most advanced students wear black belts.

Many karate-ka begin warm-ups with neck and arm rotations. A rotation is a circular motion made by a body part. Neck rotations loosen neck and shoulder muscles. Arm rotations loosen arm and shoulder muscles.

Karate-ka warm up before each workout.

Most karate-ka stretch their stomach muscles before they practice blocks. Karate-ka turn their bodies at their waists for blocking. This movement adds power to their blocks. Many karate-ka perform body stretches and upper body rotations to stretch their stomach and back muscles.

Neck and Arm Rotations

A karate-ka begins a neck rotation by tipping her head to the right. Then she slowly rolls it to the front and to the left in a circular motion. The karate-ka rolls her head from the left to the back and to the right. This completes a full neck rotation. Then she rolls her head the other way.

Arm rotations help loosen shoulder and arm muscles. The karate-ka stands with her feet about shoulder width apart. Then she swings one arm up and backward in a circle. The karate-ka then repeats the movement with her other arm. She also can swing each arm forward in a circle.

Body stretches loosen the stomach muscles.

Body Stretches and Upper Body Rotations

A karate-ka begins a body stretch while standing with her hands on her hips. Her feet are about shoulder width apart. She clasps her hands above her head and stretches her arms straight up as far as she can. Then the karate-ka slowly bends to each side.

A karate-ka does upper body rotations to stretch his stomach and hip muscles. The karate-ka stands with his feet shoulder width apart and his hands on his hips. He slowly moves his upper body to the right and back. Then he moves his upper body to the left to complete the circle.

A karate-ka moves his upper body in a circle to do an upper body rotation.

Chapter 3

Basic Blocks

Each karate-ka learns four basic blocks. They learn the rising block, the downward block, the inside block, and the outside block. Karate-ka use these basic blocks to protect their bodies from attacks.

Blocks need power to be effective. Most blocks begin on one side of the body and end on the other side. The movement from side to side adds power to blocks.

Karate-ka practice blocks with both arms. They need to be able to defend against attacks from all sides. This book describes blocks performed with the right arm.

Basic blocks protect the body from attack.

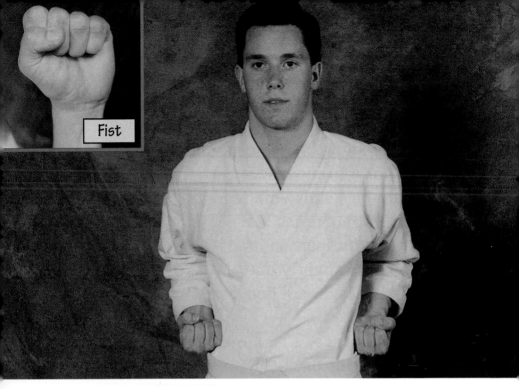

Many karate movements begin or end in the withdrawn position.

Most blocks begin or end with a fist in the withdrawn position. As the karate-ka blocks with one arm, he withdraws the other arm. In the withdrawn position, a karate-ka rests his fists by his waist slightly above the hips. The backs of his fists face the floor. His elbows point behind him.

Rising Blocks

A rising block protects the face, neck, and head from attack. A karate-ka begins a right rising

Start

Finish

A karate-ka uses a rising block to protect the face, neck, and head from attack.

block with her right leg forward. She crosses her arms over her chest with her right arm on the outside. Her arms do not touch her chest. The backs of her fists face outward. She twists her upper body to the left.

The karate-ka then pushes her right hip forward. At the same time, she quickly lifts her right arm slightly above her head. Her right arm is bent at a 45-degree angle. Her forearm passes directly in front of her face. She raises her arm and rotates her wrist. The back of her

Start

Finish

A karate-ka uses a downward block to protect the lower body and knees.

fist now faces her body. At the same time, she pulls her left fist into the withdrawn position.

Downward Blocks

A downward block protects the lower body and knees. A karate-ka begins a downward block with her right fist by her left ear. Her left arm is extended in front of her stomach. The back of the fist faces upward. She twists her upper body to the left.

The karate-ka is then ready to perform a downward block. First, she steps forward with

Start

Finish

Inside blocks stop attacks to the chest and stomach.

her right leg. She turns her upper body forward. At the same time, she swings her right arm down in front of her body. She stops her right arm slightly in front of her right leg. She pulls her left arm into the withdrawn position.

Inside Blocks and Outside Blocks
Inside blocks and outside blocks stop attacks to the chest and stomach. A karate-ka begins a right inside block with his right fist by his left hip. His right elbow points toward the floor.

His left arm is extended in front of his stomach. The back of his left fist faces upward.

Then he steps forward with his right leg. At the same time, he moves his arm in an arc to the front of his body. He rotates his forearm so the back of his fist faces away from his body. His elbow is bent at a 90-degree angle. He does not swing his right arm past his right shoulder. The karate-ka twists his upper body to the left. At the same time, he pulls his left arm into the withdrawn position.

A karate-ka begins a right outside block with his right hand behind his right ear. His right elbow points directly to the right. His left arm is straight out in front.

The karate-ka then pushes his right hip forward. He moves his bent right arm in front of his body. He twists his forearm so it faces his body. The karate-ka keeps his right forearm in front of his chest. The fist is at shoulder level. The karate-ka turns his hips to the left. At the same time, he moves his left fist into the withdrawn position.

A karate-ka moves his bent arm in front of his body for an outside block.

Chapter 4

Advanced Blocks

A karate-ka learns advanced blocks once he masters the basic blocks. Some advanced blocks include the x-block, the scooping-low block, the supporting block, and the double block.

X-Blocks

A karate-ka can use an x-block to stop a strike, punch, or kick. A karate-ka uses both arms for an x-block. She begins an upward x-block by crossing her fists in front of her chest. Her arms touch at the wrists. Then she pushes her arms upward. This allows her to block a strike or punch. She catches her opponent's arm between her hands.

The downward x-block begins with the arms crossed near the right hip. The karate-ka pushes

Advanced karate-ka learn advanced blocks such as the double block.

Start

Finish

A karate-ka pushes her arms downward for a downward x-block.

her arms downward to catch an opponent's leg between her fists. Then she can push the leg to either side. Or she can grab the leg and pull her opponent off balance.

Scooping-Low Blocks

Many karate-ka learn the scooping-low block to stop kicks. A karate-ka begins a right scooping-low block with her right arm straight out to the

Start

Finish

Many karate-ka learn scooping-low blocks to stop kicks.

side. Her left arm is in front of her. The backs of her fists face the ceiling.

Then she swings her right arm in and down. She bends her elbow at the moment her arm touches the opponent's leg. She catches the leg and scoops it up in her arm. She can hold onto the leg with her left arm and push the opponent off balance.

Start   Finish

A karate-ka uses one hand to support the blocking arm for a supporting block.

Supporting Blocks

The supporting block allows a small person to block the blows of a larger person. For a supporting block, a karate-ka uses one hand to support the blocking arm.

Most karate-ka use a supporting block with an inside block. The karate-ka performs a regular right inside block with his right arm. But his left arm changes. He uses his left hand to push the elbow of the right arm. Both arms give him more strength to push away a kick, strike, or punch.

Double blocks protect against two kinds of blows at once.

Double Blocks

Double blocks are any two blocks combined together. Double blocks protect against two kinds of blows at once. An opponent might strike or punch immediately after a kick. The karate-ka uses a double block to protect himself against these attacks.

A karate-ka might perform an inside body block using the left arm. He might add a downward block with his right arm at the same time. This combination would protect against a strike to the left and a kick to the right.

Chapter 5

Safety and Training

Safety is an important part of all karate training. Shotokan karate-ka practice low-contact karate. They practice in light-contact or no-contact situations. Students' chances of getting hurt are less in low-contact karate than in high-contact karate. Karate-ka at high-contact dojos practice in full-contact situations during training.

All karate instructors take steps to keep their students safe. Karate-ka must groom themselves. To groom means to take care of one's appearance and clothing. Karate-ka must warm up before practice. They also work to condition their bodies. To condition means to exercise daily to keep the body fit. Karate-ka

Shotokan karate-ka practice low-contact karate.

learn to control their movements. They also wear protective gear to protect themselves and others.

Grooming

Karate-ka need to keep their bodies and gi clean. This is important because sweat and dirt can spread illnesses. Karate-ka should wash before and after karate practice.

Karate-ka must trim and clean their fingernails and toenails. Long nails can scratch people. Karate-ka need to tie back long hair for practice. They might not see a kick or strike if they have hair in their faces.

Karate-ka should remove watches and jewelry before practicing. Karate-ka could hurt themselves or others if they wear jewelry. For example, karate-ka should not wear earrings. A kick or strike could tear an earring from an ear.

Warming Up and Conditioning

Karate-ka warm up before they practice. They stretch to prevent muscle injuries. Karate-ka

Karate-ka stretch to help prevent muscle injuries.

might pull muscles if they do not warm up before practicing movements.

Karate-ka condition themselves by lifting weights and jogging. Exercises strengthen their hearts, muscles, and lungs. Karate-ka stay fit to avoid hurting themselves. They can practice karate longer without becoming tired. Karate-ka can become careless when they are tired. Careless karate-ka might do a movement wrong and hurt themselves. They also could lose control of a movement and accidentally hurt someone else.

Sparring

Many karate-ka train so they can spar. To spar means to practice fighting. Two karate-ka compete in a sparring match. The person who scores the most points wins. Karate competitors must follow rules for sparring. Officials make rules to keep competitors safe.

Some karate-ka prefer low-contact sparring. They try to stop their strikes within one inch (2.5 centimeters) of their opponents.

Karate-ka who prefer high-contact sparring hit their opponents. These students still need to control their movements. They can hit their opponents only in areas that are protected with pads.

Karate-ka learn to control their movements as part of their training. They control their movements so they do not hurt themselves or other students. For example, they might tear arm muscles if they do movements the wrong

Many karate-ka train so they can spar.

way. Or they might not pay attention to where they are swinging their legs or arms. They might accidentally hit another person.

Protective Gear

Competition officials require karate-ka to wear protective gear when they spar. Karate-ka who compete in low-contact sparring matches wear mouth guards and padded gloves. A mouth guard protects the teeth. A kick or punch to the mouth could break or knock out unprotected teeth.

Padded gloves cover the hands over the knuckles. The gloves protect the hands during blocks or punches. Gloves also soften accidental blows to opponents.

Karate-ka need additional protective gear for high-contact sparring. They may wear helmets, chest protectors, forearm guards, shin guards, and foot pads. This padded gear protects the body.

The gear also protects karate-ka's bodies when they hit opponents. Karate-ka can bruise

A Shotokan karate-ka must wear a mouth guard and padded gloves to spar.

or injure their hands or feet if they hit something the wrong way.

Karate is an exciting sport to learn. But it can be dangerous if people do not follow the rules. Beginning students should not try to perform advanced movements before they master basic movements. Advanced students should continue to practice basic movements. Practice and patience will help karate-ka safely learn karate skills.

Karate is an exciting sport to learn.

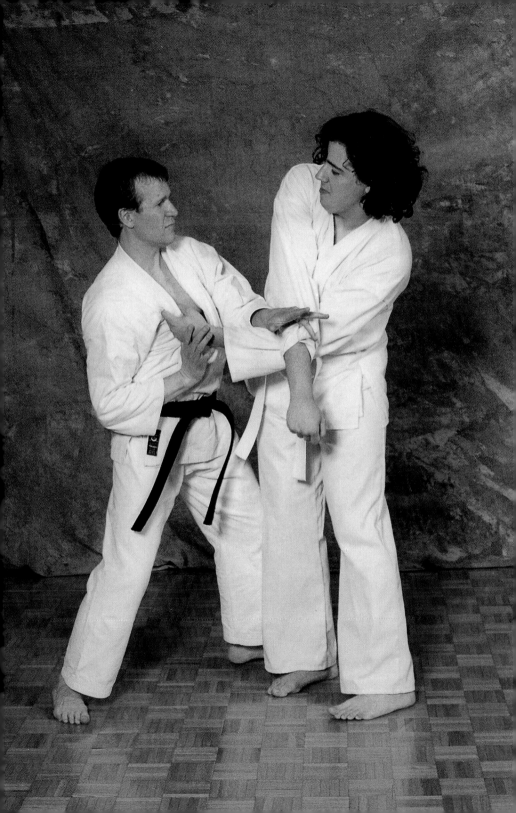

Words to Know

block (BLOK)—a karate move for defense

competition (kom-puh-TISH-uhn)—a contest of skill

condition (kuhn-DISH-uhn)—to exercise daily to keep the body fit

dojo (DOH-joh)—a karate school

gi (GEE)—a loose-fitting, cotton uniform

groom (GROOM)—to take care of appearance and clothing

injury (IN-juh-ree)—harm to the body

martial art (MAR-shuhl ART)—a style of self-defense and fighting

rotation (roh-TAY-shuhn)—a circular motion made by a body part

self-defense (SELF-di-FENSS)—the act of protecting oneself

spar (SPAHR)—to practice fighting

Karate-ka practice blocks against imaginary opponents.

To Learn More

Corrigan, Ralph. *Karate Made Easy.* New York: Sterling Publications, 1995.

Gutman, Bill. *Karate.* Minneapolis: Capstone Press, 1995.

Leder, Jane Mersky. *Karate.* Learning How. Marco, Fla.: Bancroft-Sage Publishing, 1992.

Queen, J. Allen. *Karate Basics.* New York: Sterling Publications, 1993.

Sieh, Ron. *Martial Arts for Beginners.* New York: Writers and Readers, 1995.

Karate instructors help students.

Useful Addresses

Canadian Shotokan Karate Association
1646 McPherson Drive
Port Coquitlam, BC V3C 6C9
Canada

International Society for
  Okinawan/Japanese Karate
21512 Sherman Way
Canoga Park, CA 91303

Shotokan Karate of America
2500 South La CienEga Boulevard
Los Angeles, CA 90034

World Federation Karate Organization
9506 Las Tunas Drive
Temple City, CA 91780

Internet Sites

Canadian Shotokan Karate Association
http://www.geocities.com/colosseum/field/
7270

Martial Arts Resource Page
http://www.middlebury.edu/~jswan/
martial.arts/ma.html

Shotokan Karate for Everyone
http://members.aol.com/edl12/shotokan/
index.htm

Shotokan Karate of America
http://www.ska.org/

Index